Kellogg's®
RECIPES

Publications International, Ltd.

Pictured on the back cover *(left to right):* Baked Cinnamon French Toast (*page 10*) and Corn-Crab Cakes with Chipotle Sauce (*page 30*).

ISBN: 978-1-68022-502-0

Library of Congress Control Number: 2016939329

Manufactured in China.

8 7 6 5 4 3 2 1

Microwave Cooking: Microwave ovens vary in wattage. Use the cooking times as guidelines and check for doneness before adding more time.

Preparation/Cooking Times: Preparation times are based on the approximate amount of time required to assemble the recipe before cooking, baking, chilling or serving. These times include preparation steps such as measuring, chopping and mixing. The fact that some preparations and cooking can be done simultaneously is taken into account. Preparation of optional ingredients and serving suggestions is not included.

Nutrition information for recipes can be found at www.kelloggs.com.

TABLE OF CONTENTS

BUSY-DAY BREAKFASTS

HONEY RAISIN BRAN MUFFINS

MAKES 12 MUFFINS (1 MUFFIN PER SERVING)
PREP TIME: 10 MINUTES **TOTAL TIME:** 30 MINUTES

1¾ cups all-purpose flour

1 tablespoon baking powder

¼ teaspoon salt

2 tablespoons sugar

2½ cups *Kellogg's Raisin Bran®* Cereal

1¼ cups non-fat milk

⅓ cup honey

1 egg

¼ cup vegetable oil

1 Stir together flour, baking powder, salt and sugar. Set aside.

2 In large mixing bowl, combine KELLOGG'S RAISIN BRAN cereal, milk and honey. Let stand 3 minutes or until cereal softens. Add egg and oil. Beat well. Add flour mixture, stirring only until combined. Portion batter evenly into twelve 2½-inch muffin-pan cups coated with cooking spray.

3 Bake at 400°F for 20 minutes or until lightly browned. Serve warm.

KELLOGG'S CORN FLAKES®
BANANA BREAD

MAKES 1 LOAF (16 SLICES PER LOAF)
PREP TIME: 5 MINUTES **TOTAL TIME:** 1 HOUR 30 MINUTES

2 cups all-purpose flour

1 teaspoon baking powder

½ teaspoon baking soda

½ teaspoon salt

1½ cups mashed, ripe bananas

2½ cups *Kellogg's Corn Flakes®* Cereal

½ cup margarine or butter, softened

¾ cup sugar

2 eggs

½ cup coarsely chopped walnuts

1 Stir together flour, baking powder, baking soda and salt. Set aside.

2 In medium mixing bowl, combine bananas and KELLOGG'S CORN FLAKES cereal. Let stand 5 minutes or until cereal softens. Beat well.

3 In large mixing bowl, beat margarine and sugar until combined. Add eggs. Beat well. Mix in cereal mixture and nuts. Stir in flour mixture. Spread batter evenly in 9×5×3-inch loaf pan coated with cooking spray.

4 Bake at 350°F about 1 hour or until wooden pick inserted near center comes out clean. Let cool 10 minutes before removing from pan. Cool completely before slicing. Wrap with plastic wrap.

THE ORIGINAL ALL-BRAN® MUFFINS

MAKES 12 MUFFINS (1 MUFFIN PER SERVING)

PREP TIME: 20 MINUTES **TOTAL TIME:** 50 MINUTES

1¼ cups all-purpose flour

½ cup sugar

1 tablespoon baking powder

¼ teaspoon salt

2 cups *Kellogg's® All-Bran®* Original Cereal

1¼ cups non-fat milk

1 egg

¼ cup vegetable oil

1 Stir together flour, sugar, baking powder and salt. Set aside.

2 In large mixing bowl, combine KELLOGG'S ALL-BRAN cereal and milk. Let stand about 2 minutes or until cereal softens. Add egg and oil. Beat well. Add flour mixture, stirring only until combined. Portion evenly into twelve 2½-inch muffin-pan cups coated with cooking spray.

3 Bake at 400°F about 20 minutes or until golden brown. Serve warm.

VARIATIONS

For muffins with reduced calories, fat and cholesterol, use 2 tablespoons sugar, 2 tablespoons oil and substitute 2 egg whites for 1 egg.

For muffins with reduced fat and cholesterol, substitute 2 egg whites for 1 egg and ¼ cup sweetened applesauce (or 2-ounce jar bananas baby food) for ¼ cup vegetable oil. (Muffin texture may vary slightly from The Original ALL-BRAN Muffins recipe.)

BAKED CINNAMON FRENCH TOAST

MAKES 4 SERVINGS | **PREP TIME:** 15 MINUTES **TOTAL TIME:** 35 MINUTES

3 eggs, slightly beaten

⅔ cup non-fat milk or evaporated non-fat milk

2 tablespoons sugar, divided

1½ teaspoons vanilla extract

¾ teaspoon cinnamon, divided

8 slices (1-inch-thick) French or Italian bread, about 3 to 4 inches in diameter

1 cup *Kellogg's® Rice Krispies®* Cereal

2 medium bananas, sliced or 2 cups sliced fresh strawberries

½ cup maple syrup, warmed

1 In shallow dish, stir together eggs, milk, 1 tablespoon sugar, vanilla and ½ teaspoon cinnamon. Dip bread slices into egg mixture, turning to generously coat both sides. Place on 15×10×1-inch baking pan coated with cooking spray.

2 Bake at 450°F about 11 minutes or until light brown.

3 Meanwhile, in small bowl, stir together remaining 1 tablespoon sugar and remaining ¼ teaspoon cinnamon.

4 Turn bread slices. Sprinkle with KELLOGG'S RICE KRISPIES cereal. Lightly press cereal into bread. Sprinkle sugar-cinnamon mixture over cereal. Bake at 450°F about 5 minutes more or until light brown.

5 Top each slice with banana slices. Serve with syrup.

APPLE CINNAMON QUICK BREAD

MAKES 1 LOAF (16 SERVINGS)
PREP TIME: 10 MINUTES **TOTAL TIME:** 1 HOUR 5 MINUTES

1½ cups *Keebler®* Grahams Cinnamon Crisp Crackers, finely crushed

1½ cups all-purpose flour

¼ cup sugar

1 tablespoon baking powder

1 teaspoon salt

2 eggs, beaten

1 cup milk

⅓ cup vegetable oil

1 cup peeled chopped apples (1 large)

1 In large bowl, stir together KEEBLER cracker crumbs, flour, sugar, baking powder and salt.

2 In small bowl, combine eggs, milk and oil. Add to cracker mixture. Stir until just combined. Fold in apple.

3 Spread in greased 8×4×2-inch loaf pan. Bake at 350°F for 55 to 60 minutes or until toothpick inserted near center comes out clean.

4 Cool in pan on wire rack for 10 minutes. Remove from pan. Cool completely.

SPICY RAISIN MUFFINS

MAKES 6 SERVINGS (1 MUFFIN PER SERVING)
PREP TIME: 10 MINUTES **TOTAL TIME:** 40 MINUTES

2 cups all-purpose flour

½ teaspoon salt

2 tablespoons baking powder

1 teaspoon pumpkin pie spice (optional)

4½ cups *Kellogg's Raisin Bran®* **Cereal**

¼ cup firmly packed brown sugar

2 cups non-fat milk

3 egg whites

3 tablespoons vegetable oil

1 Stir together flour, salt, baking powder and spice; set aside.

2 Combine KELLOGG'S RAISIN BRAN cereal, brown sugar and milk into large mixing bowl. Stir to combine. Let stand 2 minutes or until cereal absorbs milk. Add egg whites and oil; beat well.

3 Add flour mixture to cereal mixture, stirring only until combined. Using ⅔ cup batter for each muffin, portion batter into 6 paper-lined 2¾-inch muffin-pan cups.

4 Bake in 375°F oven about 28 minutes or until golden brown. Serve hot.

GRIDDLE CAKES

MAKES 4 SERVINGS | PREP TIME: 15 MINUTES **TOTAL TIME:** 30 MINUTES

2 cups all-purpose flour

1 tablespoon baking powder

1 teaspoon baking soda

1 teaspoon salt

3 tablespoons sugar

1 cup *Kellogg's® All-Bran®* Original or 1 cup *Kellogg's® All-Bran® Bran Buds®* Cereal

1 cup hot water

1 egg

1½ cups milk

1 Stir together flour, baking powder, baking soda, salt and sugar. Set aside.

2 Combine KELLOGG'S ALL-BRAN cereal and hot water. Let stand about 2 minutes or until cereal softens.

3 In large mixing bowl, beat egg and milk. Stir in cereal mixture. Add flour mixture, stirring only until combined.

4 Bake pancakes on preheated griddle at 375°F until browned on both sides, turning only once. Serve with brown sugar, maple syrup, honey or jelly, if desired.

ORANGE COFFEE CAKE

MAKES 9 SERVINGS | PREP TIME: 30 MINUTES **TOTAL TIME:** 1 HOUR

2 tablespoons margarine or butter, softened

⅓ cup all-purpose flour

½ cup firmly packed brown sugar

1 tablespoon grated orange peel

CAKE

1¼ cups sifted cake flour

2 teaspoons baking powder

½ teaspoon salt

¼ cup shortening

½ cup granulated sugar

1 egg

2 teaspoons grated orange peel

⅛ teaspoon almond extract

½ cup *Kellogg's® All-Bran®* Original Cereal

¼ cup orange juice

¼ cup milk

1 Using pastry blender, cut margarine into the ⅓ cup flour, brown sugar and the 1 tablespoon orange peel until mixture resembles coarse crumbs. Set aside for topping.

2 Sift together cake flour, baking powder and salt. Set aside.

3 In large mixing bowl, beat shortening and granulated sugar until thoroughly combined. Add egg, the 2 teaspoons orange peel and almond extract. Beat well. Stir in KELLOGG'S ALL-BRAN cereal, orange juice and milk. Add flour mixture, stirring only until combined. Spread evenly in 9×9×2-inch baking pan coated with cooking spray. Sprinkle with topping, pressing lightly into batter.

4 Bake at 375°F about 25 minutes or until wooden pick inserted in center comes out clean. Cut into squares and serve hot.

MARVELOUS MAPLE GRANOLA

MAKES 18 SERVINGS (½ CUP PER SERVING)
PREP TIME: 10 MINUTES **TOTAL TIME:** 55 MINUTES

¾ cup maple syrup
¼ cup vegetable oil
¼ cup honey
1 teaspoon vanilla
¼ teaspoon salt
2 cups *Kellogg's® Frosted Flakes®* Cereal

2 cups old-fashioned rolled oats
1 cup slivered almonds
1 cup flaked coconut
1 cup dried tart cherries or raisins
Yogurt or fresh fruit

1 In small bowl, stir together syrup, oil, honey, vanilla and salt.

2 In large bowl, combine KELLOGG'S FROSTED FLAKES cereal, oats, almonds and coconut. Drizzle syrup mixture over top. Gently stir until coated. Evenly spread in 15×10×1-inch baking pan lined with foil and lightly coated with cooking spray.

3 Bake at 325°F for 40 to 45 minutes or until golden brown, stirring every 10 minutes. Cool completely, stirring once or twice. Stir in cherries. Store in airtight container for up to 2 weeks.

4 Serve sprinkled over yogurt or fresh fruit.

BANANA MUFFINS

MAKES 12 SERVINGS | PREP TIME: 25 MINUTES **TOTAL TIME:** 1 HOUR

1¼ cups all-purpose flour

1 tablespoon baking powder

½ teaspoon salt

½ teaspoon cinnamon

¼ teaspoon nutmeg

½ cup firmly packed brown sugar

2 cups *Kellogg's Corn Flakes®* Cereal

1 egg

⅓ cup non-fat milk

¼ cup vegetable oil

1 cup mashed, ripe bananas

1 Stir together flour, baking powder, salt, spices, brown sugar and KELLOGG'S CORN FLAKES cereal. Set aside.

2 In large mixing bowl, combine egg, milk and oil. Stir in bananas. Add flour mixture, stirring only until combined. Portion evenly into twelve 2½-inch muffin-pan cups coated with cooking spray.

3 Bake at 400°F about 20 minutes or until lightly browned. Serve warm.

TIP

For the best banana flavor, make sure your bananas are very ripe.

BRAN WAFFLES

MAKES 4 SERVINGS | PREP TIME: 15 MINUTES **TOTAL TIME:** 25 MINUTES

¾ cup all-purpose flour

¼ cup sugar

1 teaspoon baking powder

½ teaspoon baking soda

¼ teaspoon salt

1 cup *Kellogg's® All-Bran®* Original Cereal

2 eggs, separated

1 cup buttermilk or sour milk

6 tablespoons melted margarine or butter

1 In large mixing bowl, stir together flour, sugar, baking powder, baking soda, salt and KELLOGG'S ALL-BRAN cereal. Slightly beat egg yolks. Add egg yolks, buttermilk and melted margarine to cereal mixture. Stir until well blended.

2 In small mixing bowl, beat egg whites until stiff peaks form. Fold into batter.

3 Bake in preheated waffle iron according to manufacturer's directions or until steaming stops and waffle is golden brown. Serve hot with syrup or fruit topping, if desired.

SPECIAL K® PARFAIT ▶

MAKES 2 SERVINGS | **PREP TIME:** 5 MINUTES **TOTAL TIME:** 5 MINUTES

1 (8-ounce) container low-fat vanilla flavored yogurt

1 cup fresh fruit (sliced strawberries, sliced banana, blueberries or raspberries)

1 cup *Kellogg's® Special K®* Cereal Original

1 In 2 tall glasses, layer yogurt, fruit and SPECIAL K cereal until glass is full.

2 Top with extra fruit.

3 Serve immediately.

PEACH SMOOTHIE

MAKES 4 SERVINGS | **PREP TIME:** 5 MINUTES **TOTAL TIME:** 5 MINUTES

2 cups unsweetened frozen sliced peaches

½ cup non-fat plain yogurt

½ cup non-fat milk

½ cup sugar

4 cups *Kellogg's® Special K®* Red Berries Crispy Rice Cereal

Place peaches, yogurt, milk and sugar in food processor or blender container. Using metal blade, process until smooth, scrapping container occasionally. Serve over KELLOGG'S SPECIAL K cereal.

DINNER WINNERS

SPICY TOMATO MINI-LOAVES

MAKES 6 SERVINGS | PREP TIME: 30 MINUTES **TOTAL TIME:** 1 HOUR 5 MINUTES

3 cups *Kellogg's Corn Flakes® Cereal*

1 (10¾-ounce) can condensed tomato soup, divided

¼ cup finely chopped onions

1 egg

1 tablespoon horseradish (optional)

1½ pounds lean ground beef

2 tablespoons firmly packed brown sugar

1 teaspoon prepared mustard

Parsley (optional)

1 In large mixing bowl, combine KELLOGG'S CORN FLAKES cereal, ½ cup of the tomato soup, onion, egg and horseradish. Mix in ground beef. Portion meat mixture and shape into 6 individual loaves or ovals. Place on foil-lined baking sheet.

2 In small bowl, mix together remaining soup, brown sugar and mustard. Spread evenly over meat loaves.

3 Bake at 350°F about 35 minutes or until meat is cooked. Serve hot garnished with parsley, if desired.

CORN-CRAB CAKES WITH CHIPOTLE SAUCE

MAKES 2 SERVINGS | PREP TIME: 10 MINUTES **TOTAL TIME:** 15 MINUTES

3 tablespoons mayonnaise

¾ teaspoon chipotle hot pepper sauce, divided

1 egg, slightly beaten

⅓ cup *Kellogg's®* Corn Flake Crumbs, divided

¼ cup fresh or frozen corn

2 tablespoons sliced green onions

1 teaspoon Dijon mustard

½ teaspoon coriander

1 (6-ounce) can crabmeat, drained, flaked and cartilage removed

2 teaspoons butter or margarine

1 In small bowl, stir together mayonnaise and ½ teaspoon pepper sauce. Cover and refrigerate until serving time.

2 In medium bowl, stir together egg, ¼ cup KELLOGG'S Corn Flake crumbs, corn, onion, mustard, coriander and remaining ¼ teaspoon pepper sauce. Add crabmeat. Mix well. Shape into four ½-inch thick patties.

3 Place remaining crumbs in shallow dish. Lightly press patties into crumbs, coating both sides.

4 In large nonstick skillet, cook patties in hot butter about 4 minutes or until golden brown, turning once. Serve with mayonnaise mixture.

DINNER WINNERS

CRUNCHY ORANGE FISH FILLETS

MAKES 4 SERVINGS | PREP TIME: 20 MINUTES **TOTAL TIME:** 45 MINUTES

1 pound fish fillets, fresh or frozen thawed

2 cups *Kellogg's® Special K®* Cereal Original

½ teaspoon grated orange peel

½ teaspoon salt

¼ teaspoon dried tarragon leaves

⅛ teaspoon pepper

¼ teaspoon chopped parsley

¼ cup reduced-calorie margarine, melted

1 Pat fish fillets with paper towel. Set aside.

2 Place KELLOGG'S SPECIAL K cereal in shallow dish or pan. Stir in orange peel, salt, tarragon, pepper and parsley.

3 Dip fish fillets in melted margarine. Coat with cereal mixture. Place in single layer in foil-lined shallow baking pan.

4 Bake at 375°F about 25 minutes or until fish flakes easily with a fork. Do not cover or turn fish while baking. Serve with orange slices.

FAVORITE MEATLOAF

MAKES 8 SERVINGS (1 SLICE PER SERVING)
PREP TIME: 10 MINUTES **TOTAL TIME:** 1 HOUR 15 MINUTES

3 cups *Kellogg's® Special K®* Cereal Original
1½ pounds lean ground beef
1 egg, slightly beaten
½ cup finely chopped onions
½ cup finely cut celery
½ cup cooked tomatoes
½ cup non-fat milk
1½ teaspoons salt
⅛ teaspoon pepper

1 In medium mixing bowl, combine all ingredients, mixing well. Pack lightly in ungreased 9×5×3-inch loaf pan.

2 Bake at 375°F about 1 hour. Let stand 5 minutes before turning out onto heated platter. Slice and serve immediately.

DINNER WINNERS

SALMON WITH FLAKES AND ALMOND TOPPING

MAKES 4 SERVINGS | PREP TIME: 25 MINUTES **TOTAL TIME:** 33 MINUTES

½ cup *Kellogg's Corn Flakes*® Cereal

¼ cup chopped almonds

¼ cup butter, softened

¼ cup snipped fresh basil

2 tablespoons grated Parmesan cheese

1 teaspoon grated lemon peel

2 cloves garlic, minced

¼ teaspoon pepper

4 salmon fillets, skinned (about 6 ounces each)

Steamed spinach (optional)

1 Coarsely crush KELLOGG'S CORN FLAKES cereal. In a small bowl, combine almonds, butter, basil, Parmesan cheese, lemon peel, garlic, and pepper; stir in cereal. Rinse fish; pat dry. Measure thickness of fish. Place fish on the greased rack of a broiler pan. Spoon cereal mixture on top of fillets; pat gently to spread.

2 Bake at 400°F for 4 to 6 minutes per ½-inch thickness or until fish flakes easily with a fork. For food safety, the internal temperature of the fish should be a minimum of 145°F. Serve each piece of fish over steamed spinach, if desired.

FAMILY TUNA CASSEROLE

MAKES 6 SERVINGS | **PREP TIME:** 15 MINUTES **TOTAL TIME:** 45 MINUTES

1½ cups *Kellogg's® All-Bran® Complete®* Wheat Flakes Cereal, divided

2 teaspoons butter or margarine, melted

1 cup shredded American cheese (4 ounces), divided

1 (6½-ounce) can chunk light tuna in water, well-drained and flaked

1 (10½-ounce) can condensed cream of mushroom soup

⅓ cup non-fat milk

2 cups egg noodles, cooked and drained

½ cup cooked peas

½ cup thinly sliced celery

2 tablespoons chopped pimientos

1 In small mixing bowl, toss 1 cup KELLOGG'S ALL-BRAN COMPLETE cereal and butter. Set aside for topping. Set aside ½ cup of the cheese.

2 Stir together remaining cereal, remaining cheese, tuna, soup and milk in large mixing bowl. Stir in noodles, peas, celery and pimientos. Spread in 10×6×2-inch (1½-quart) glass baking dish. Sprinkle with cereal topping.

3 Bake at 350°F for 25 minutes. Top with reserved cheese. Bake about 5 minutes longer or until cheese melts and tuna mixture is thoroughly heated.

TANGY TURKEY SPINACH SALAD

MAKES 4 SERVINGS | PREP TIME: 15 MINUTES **TOTAL TIME:** 45 MINUTES

¼ cup honey

¼ cup cider vinegar

2 tablespoons reduced-sodium soy sauce

1 teaspoon Dijon mustard

1 pound turkey breast tenderloin

2 egg whites, slightly beaten

2 cups *Kellogg's® Special K®* Low-Fat Granola

2 tablespoons butter or margarine, melted

6 cups torn fresh spinach

1 (11-ounce) can mandarin orange sections, drained

½ cup thinly sliced celery

½ cup chopped, seeded cucumber

2 green onions, thinly sliced

1 In small bowl, whisk together honey, vinegar, soy sauce and mustard. Cover and refrigerate until needed.

2 If necessary, lightly pound tenderloin to 1-inch thickness. Dip into egg whites. Roll in KELLOGG'S SPECIAL K cereal. Place on baking sheet lined with foil and coated with cooking spray. Drizzle with butter.

3 Bake at 350°F for 25 to 30 minutes or until turkey is tender and no longer pink.

4 Meanwhile, in large bowl, toss together spinach, oranges, celery, cucumber and onions. Arrange on 4 serving plates.

5 Carefully slice hot turkey. Place on salads. Drizzle honey mixture over top. Serve immediately.

GRILLED BLACK BEAN AND PORK BURRITOS

MAKES 8 SERVINGS | **PREP TIME:** 1 HOUR 15 MINUTES **TOTAL TIME:** 1 HOUR 25 MINUTES

4 cups water*

1 pound lean pork stew meat*

1 medium onion, quartered*

2 cloves garlic*

1 (15-ounce) can black beans, rinsed and drained

1 cup *Kellogg's Corn Flakes*® Cereal, crushed to ½ cup

1 (4-ounce) can diced green chili peppers, drained

1 teaspoon cumin

⅔ cup salsa

1½ cups shredded reduced-fat sharp Cheddar cheese

½ cup sliced green onions

8 flour tortillas (9- to 10-inch)

Salsa (optional)

Fat-free sour cream (optional)

1 In Dutch oven, combine water, pork, onion and garlic. Bring to boiling; reduce heat. Simmer, covered, for 45 minutes or until pork is tender. Drain meat. Discard onion and garlic.

2 Cool meat slightly. Use two forks to shred meat, discarding any fat or cartilage. (If desired, cover and refrigerate for up to 2 days.)

3 Use back of spoon to slightly mash beans. Stir in KELLOGG'S CORN FLAKES cereal, chile peppers and cumin. Set aside.

4 In medium bowl, stir together pork and salsa. Spread bean mixture on tortillas. Top with pork mixture, cheese and onions. Fold tortilla edges over filling. Fold in sides. Roll-up, completely enclosing filling. Secure with toothpicks.

5 Grill filled tortillas on grill rack directly over medium-low heat about 7 minutes or until lightly browned, turning once. Remove toothpicks. Serve with salsa and sour cream, if desired.

TIP

Serve these great-tasting burritos at your next patio party. Cook and chill the pork up to 2 days in advance. At party time, set the pork mixture, bean mixture, cheese and tortillas out. Guests can make their own burritos.

*NOTE

If desired, substitute 2 cups shredded cooked pork or chicken for the water, stew meat, onion and garlic. Omit step 1 of the directions. Continue as directed above, starting with step 2.

OVEN-CRUSTY FISH

MAKES 4 SERVINGS | PREP TIME: 15 MINUTES **TOTAL TIME:** 35 MINUTES

4 cups *Kellogg's Corn Flakes®* **Cereal, crushed to 1 cup, or 1 cup** *Kellogg's®* **Corn Flake Crumbs**

1 pound fish fillets, fresh or frozen, thawed

½ cup milk

1 tablespoon salt

4 teaspoons vegetable oil or melted margarine

1 Place KELLOGG'S CORN FLAKES cereal in shallow dish. Set aside.

2 Cut fish into serving pieces allowing about ¼ pound for each serving.

3 Combine milk and salt in small dish. Dip fish in milk, then in cereal to coat. Place on shallow baking pan coated well with cooking spray or lined with foil and coated with cooking spray. Drizzle fish with vegetable oil.

4 Bake at 375°F about 20 minutes or until fish flakes and is done. Serve hot.

MEDITERRANEAN STUFFED CHICKEN BREASTS

MAKES 4 SERVINGS | **PREP TIME:** 25 MINUTES **TOTAL TIME:** 50 MINUTES

4 large boneless, skinless chicken breast halves (about 1 pound)

¼ teaspoon garlic salt

¼ teaspoon pepper

4 ounces goat cheese (¾ cup)

3 tablespoons snipped oil-packed sun-dried tomatoes, drained

2 tablespoons chopped, pitted Greek-style olives

½ cup low-fat buttermilk

1 teaspoon dried oregano leaves, crushed

½ teaspoon smoked paprika or paprika

2½ cups *Kellogg's Corn Flakes®* Cereal

Steamed green beans tossed with butter (optional)

1 Place each breast half between 2 pieces of plastic wrap. Working from center to edges, pound lightly with flat side of meat mallet to ¼-inch thickness. Remove plastic wrap. Season with garlic salt and pepper.

2 In small bowl, stir together goat cheese, tomatoes and olives. Divide mixture among chicken breasts. For each, fold chicken around filling to form a mound; fasten with wooden toothpick. Repeat with remaining chicken.

3 In shallow bowl, combine buttermilk, oregano and paprika. Dip chicken into buttermilk, covering all sides, and coat with KELLOGG'S CORN FLAKES cereal.

4 Place chicken on 17×11×1-inch baking sheet coated with cooking spray. Bake at 375°F for 25 to 30 minutes or until chicken is tender and no longer pink. For food safety, internal temperature of the chicken should reach at least 165°F. Remove toothpicks before serving. Serve with green beans, if desired.

TIP

Dress up chicken breasts with stir-together sun-dried tomato and olive filling and a crispy herbed coating.

SAUCY STROGANOFF

MAKES 6 (1-CUP) SERVINGS | **PREP TIME:** 40 MINUTES **TOTAL TIME:** 50 MINUTES

2 cubes beef bouillon

¾ cup boiling water

3 tablespoons ketchup

1 tablespoon prepared mustard

¼ cup chopped onions

¼ teaspoon liquid hot pepper sauce

2 cups *Kellogg's Corn Flakes®* Cereal, crushed to ½ cup

1 egg

1½ pounds lean ground beef

½ cup boiling water

1 (10¾-ounce) can low-sodium condensed cream of mushroom soup

1 cup sour cream

2 teaspoons Worcestershire sauce

1 (3-ounce) can sliced mushrooms, drained

¼ teaspoon dry minced garlic

1 tablespoon dried parsley flakes, divided

Hot cooked noodles or rice

1 In large mixing bowl, dissolve 1 bouillon cube in the ¾ cup water. Add next 6 ingredients. Beat well. Add ground beef. Mix until combined. Portion meat mixture, using level tablespoon. Shape into meatballs. Place in single layer in shallow baking pan, coated with cooking spray or foil lined.

2 Bake at 400°F about 15 minutes or until well browned.

3 In 2-quart saucepan, dissolve remaining bouillon cube in the ½ cup water. Stir in soup, sour cream, Worcestershire sauce, mushrooms, garlic and 2 teaspoons of the parsley flakes. Cook over medium heat, stirring frequently, until sauce is thoroughly heated. Add meatballs. Cook until thoroughly heated. Serve meatballs over hot cooked noodles or rice. Sprinkle with remaining 1 teaspoon parsley flakes. Serve hot.

SOUTHWEST STUFFED PEPPERS

MAKES 6 SERVINGS | **PREP TIME:** 30 MINUTES **TOTAL TIME:** 1 HOUR

6 large green bell peppers

1 pound lean ground beef

1 medium onion, sliced

2 cups *Kellogg's® Rice Krispies®* or 2 cups *Kellogg's Corn Flakes®* Cereal

⅛ teaspoon minced garlic

2 teaspoons chili powder

1 teaspoon chili powder

1 teaspoon salt

⅛ teaspoon salt

1 (2¼-ounce) can sliced ripe olives, drained

1 (6-ounce) can tomato paste

1 (14½-ounce) can whole peeled tomatoes, drained

½ cup shredded sharp Cheddar cheese

1 Wash peppers. Cut off tops and remove seedy portions. Precook in large amount of boiling water about 5 minutes. Drain well. Place peppers, cut side up, in shallow baking pan coated with cooking spray. Set aside.

2 In 12-inch skillet, cook ground beef and onion until meat is browned, stirring frequently. Drain off drippings. Add remaining ingredients, except cheese. Stir to combine, cutting tomatoes into pieces with spoon. Remove from heat. Spoon into peppers, dividing evenly.

3 Bake at 350°F about 25 minutes or until filling is thoroughly heated. Remove from oven. Sprinkle with cheese. Return to oven. Bake about 5 minutes longer or until cheese melts. Serve hot.

MICROWAVE DIRECTIONS

1 Wash peppers. Cut off tops and remove seedy portions. Lightly salt inside of each pepper. Place peppers, cut side up, in 12×7 ½×2-inch (2-quart) glass baking dish. Set aside.

2 Place ground beef and onion in 8×8×2-inch (1½-quart) glass baking dish. Stir to crumble. Microwave on HIGH 6 to 7 minutes or until beef is cooked, stirring occasionally. Drain off drippings. Add remaining ingredients except cheese. Stir to combine, cutting tomatoes into pieces with spoon. Spoon filling into peppers, dividing evenly. Cover stuffed pepper with plastic wrap. Poke several holes in plastic wrap to allow steam to escape.

3 Microwave on HIGH about 15 minutes or until filling is thoroughly heated and peppers are tender. Sprinkle tops with cheese. Microwave on HIGH until cheese melts.

DINNER WINNERS

TO CLOSE

ON THE SIDE

STUFFED MUSHROOMS

MAKES 4 SERVINGS | **PREP TIME:** 20 MINUTES **TOTAL TIME:** 50 MINUTES

1 cup *Sunshine® Cheez-It®* Original Crackers, finely crushed

½ teaspoon salt

1⁄16 teaspoon pepper

1 pound large mushrooms

⅓ cup minced onions

⅓ cup minced celery

⅓ cup butter

3 tablespoons minced parsley

1 Mix SUNSHINE CHEEZ-IT crumbs with salt and pepper. Set aside.

2 Clean mushrooms and save stems for later use in soups and sauces. Sauté onions and celery in butter until soft; do not brown. Remove from heat; stir in parsley and crumbs. Stuff into mushroom caps.

3 Place caps, stuffed-side up, in shallow pan. Pour enough water in bottom of pan to come up about ¼ the depth of the mushroom caps. Bake in 450°F oven for 25 to 30 minutes or until mushrooms are tender but not mushy.

HERBED BAKED TOMATOES

MAKES 8 SERVINGS | **PREP TIME:** 10 MINUTES **TOTAL TIME:** 40 MINUTES

4 medium tomatoes (about 3 inches in diameter)

2 tablespoons chopped fresh basil

1 tablespoon chopped fresh rosemary

¼ teaspoon coarse ground pepper

2 teaspoons butter or margarine, melted

1 cup *Kellogg's Corn Flakes®* Cereal

3 tablespoons finely shredded Parmesan cheese

1 Remove stems and cores from tomatoes. Crosswise cut tomatoes in half. Place, cut-side up, in 12×8×2-inch baking dish. Sprinkle tops with basil, rosemary and pepper. Cover with foil. Bake at 350°F for 25 minutes.

2 Meanwhile, in small bowl, drizzle butter over KELLOGG'S CORN FLAKES cereal. Add cheese. Toss to coat. Remove foil from tomatoes. Sprinkle cereal mixture on top. Bake, uncovered, about 5 minutes or until cereal mixture is crisp.

CREAMY GREEN BEAN CASSEROLE

MAKES 8 SERVINGS | PREP TIME: 20 MINUTES **TOTAL TIME:** 40 MINUTES

¼ cup margarine or butter, divided

2 cups *Kellogg's Corn Flakes®* Cereal, crushed to 1½ cups

2 tablespoons all-purpose flour

¼ teaspoon salt

¼ teaspoon pepper

1 teaspoon sugar

1½ teaspoons onion powder

1 cup low-fat sour cream

1 (20-ounce) package French-style green beans, cooked and drained

1 cup shredded low-fat Swiss cheese (4 ounces)

1 In 3-quart saucepan, melt margarine over low heat. Remove from heat. Remove 2 tablespoons margarine and mix with KELLOGG'S CORN FLAKES cereal. Set aside for topping.

2 To remaining margarine in pan, stir in flour, salt, pepper, sugar and onion powder. Gradually stir in sour cream. Fold in green beans. Pour into 10×6×2-inch (1½-quart) glass baking dish coated with cooking spray. Sprinkle cheese and cereal mixture over casserole.

3 Bake at 400°F about 20 minutes or until thoroughly heated. Serve hot.

CREAMY SPINACH BAKE

MAKES 6 SERVINGS | **PREP TIME:** 30 MINUTES **TOTAL TIME:** 1 HOUR

5 tablespoons margarine or butter, divided

3 cups *Kellogg's Corn Flakes®* Cereal, crushed to 1½ cups, divided

2 tablespoons all-purpose flour

¼ teaspoon salt

3 tablespoons chopped onions

1¼ cups non-fat milk

1 cup shredded, low-fat Swiss cheese (4 ounces)

1 (10-ounce) package chopped frozen leaf spinach, thawed and drained

2 eggs, well beaten

1 In 3-quart saucepan, melt margarine over low heat. Remove 2 tablespoons and mix with ¾ cup of the KELLOGG'S CORN FLAKES cereal. Set aside for topping.

2 To remaining margarine in pan, stir in flour, salt and onion. Cook and stir about 1 minute. Add milk, stirring until smooth. Increase heat to medium and cook until mixture boils, stirring constantly. Remove from heat.

3 Add cheese to hot sauce, stirring until slightly melted. Stir in spinach, eggs and ¾ cup cereal. Spread mixture in shallow 1-quart casserole dish. Sprinkle cereal topping on spinach mixture.

4 Bake at 350°F about 25 minutes or until thoroughly heated. Serve hot.

ON THE SIDE

BAKED POTATOES WITH SOUR CREAM

MAKES 8 SERVINGS | PREP TIME: 20 MINUTES **TOTAL TIME:** 45 MINUTES

⅔ cup chopped onions

2 tablespoons margarine or butter

1½ cups sour cream

2 eggs, slightly beaten

4 cups sliced cooked potatoes or shredded hashbrown potatoes

½ teaspoon salt

⅛ teaspoon pepper

2 cups *Kellogg's Corn Flakes®* Cereal, crushed to ½ cup, or ½ cup *Kellogg's®* Corn Flake Crumbs

¼ cup shredded Cheddar cheese

1 tablespoon margarine or butter, melted

1 In 1-quart saucepan, cook onions in the 2 tablespoons margarine until golden brown, stirring frequently. Set aside.

2 In small mixing bowl, combine sour cream and eggs. Set aside.

3 Place half the potatoes in lightly greased 10×6×2-inch (1½-quart) glass baking dish. Spread half the onions over potatoes and pour half the sour cream mixture on top. Repeat using remaining potatoes, onions and sour cream mixture. Sprinkle with salt and pepper.

4 In medium mixing bowl, combine KELLOGG'S CORN FLAKES cereal, cheese and the 1 tablespoon melted margarine. Sprinkle cereal mixture over potatoes.

5 Bake at 350°F about 25 minutes or until top is golden brown. Serve hot.

ON THE SIDE

SPINACH-FETA BAKE

MAKES 6 (SIDE-DISH) OR 4 (MAIN-DISH) SERVINGS
PREP TIME: 20 MINUTES **TOTAL TIME:** 1 HOUR 10 MINUTES

½ cup chopped onion

3 cloves garlic, minced

1 teaspoon olive oil

2 (10-ounce) packages frozen chopped spinach, thawed

1 cup shredded carrots

1 cup low-fat cottage cheese, drained

1 cup crumbled feta cheese (4 ounces)

¾ cup *Kellogg's Corn Flakes*® Cereal, crushed and divided

½ cup refrigerated egg substitute*

¼ cup finely shredded Parmesan cheese

2 tablespoons chopped fresh oregano or 2 teaspoons dried oregano leaves

½ teaspoon coarse ground black pepper

*If desired, substitute 2 lightly beaten eggs for the egg substitute.

1 In small saucepan, cook onion and garlic in oil until tender.

2 Place spinach in colander. Firmly press with back of spoon to remove excess moisture. In medium bowl, stir together onion mixture, spinach, carrots, cottage cheese, feta cheese, ½ cup crushed KELLOGG'S CORN FLAKES cereal, egg substitute, Parmesan cheese, oregano and pepper.

3 Spoon into 1½-quart casserole dish coated with cooking spray. Sprinkle remaining ¼ cup cereal over spinach mixture. Bake at 350°F for 50 minutes or until knife inserted near center comes out clean.

ON THE SIDE

LEMONY APPLE SALAD

MAKES 6 SERVINGS | PREP TIME: 10 MINUTES **TOTAL TIME:** 10 MINUTES

½ cup lemon low-fat yogurt

1 tablespoon finely snipped fresh parsley

2 cups cubed, unpeeled red apples (2 medium)

½ cup thinly sliced celery

½ cup seedless red grapes, halved

½ cup *Kellogg's® All-Bran® Original* or ½ cup *Kellogg's® All-Bran® Bran Buds®* Cereal

6 lettuce leaves

1 In medium bowl, combine yogurt and parsley. Stir in apples, celery and grapes. Cover and refrigerate until ready to serve.

2 Just before serving, stir in KELLOGG'S ALL-BRAN cereal. Serve on lettuce leaves.

ON THE SIDE

FRESH POTATO-CARROT CASSEROLE

MAKES 6 SERVINGS | PREP TIME: 25 MINUTES **TOTAL TIME:** 50 MINUTES

2 teaspoons margarine or butter

1 cup *Kellogg's® All-Bran® Complete®* Wheat Flakes Cereal, divided

⅛ teaspoon ground thyme

1½ cups sliced potatoes (about ½ pound)

1½ cups sliced carrots (about ½ pounds)

2 tablespoons margarine or butter

5 teaspoons all-purpose flour

½ teaspoon salt

Dash pepper

⅛ teaspoon rosemary leaves

1 cup non-fat milk

1 Melt the 2 teaspoons margarine. Stir in ¾ cup of the KELLOGG'S ALL-BRAN COMPLETE cereal and the thyme. Set aside for topping.

2 Place potatoes and carrots in medium saucepan with salted water to cover. Bring to a boil. Boil, uncovered, for 5 minutes. Remove from heat. Drain.

3 Melt the 2 tablespoons margarine in large saucepan over low heat. Stir in flour, salt, pepper and rosemary. Add milk gradually, stirring until smooth. Increase heat to medium and cook until mixture boils and thickens, stirring constantly. Remove from heat.

4 Gently stir in potatoes, carrots and remaining ¼ cup KELLOGG'S COMPLETE ALL-BRAN cereal. Pour into 1½-quart round casserole. Sprinkle with cereal topping.

5 Bake at 350°F about 25 minutes or until vegetables are tender.

ON THE SIDE

CRISPY STUFFED SUMMER SQUASH

MAKES 4 SERVINGS | **PREP TIME:** 20 MINUTES **TOTAL TIME:** 35 MINUTES

2 medium zucchini or yellow summer squash

1 egg, beaten

1 cup *Keebler® Zesta®* Original Crackers, coarsely crushed

3 slices bacon, crisp-cooked, drained, crumbled

2 tablespoons finely chopped carrots

2 tablespoons margarine or butter, melted

1 tablespoon finely chopped onions

1 teaspoon celery seeds

1⅜ teaspoons dried sage leaves

¼ teaspoon pepper

2 tablespoons shredded Cheddar cheese

1 Lengthwise halve zucchini or squash. Use spoon to scoop out centers, leaving ¼-inch shell. In medium bowl, stir together egg, KEEBLER ZESTA crackers, bacon, carrots, margarine, onion, celery seeds, sage and pepper. Spoon into zucchini or squash. Place in shallow baking dish. Cover with foil.

2 Bake at 350°F for 10 minutes. Remove foil. Bake at 350°F about 20 minutes more or until zucchini is tender. Sprinkle with cheese. Let stand for 2 minutes or until cheese melts.

ON THE SIDE

TURKEY SAUSAGE STUFFING

MAKES 6 SERVINGS | PREP TIME: 20 MINUTES **TOTAL TIME:** 1 HOUR 5 MINUTES

8 ounces lean turkey
sausages

⅔ cup chopped onions

1½ cups chopped celery

1 tablespoon chopped
parsley

½ teaspoon salt

¼ teaspoon pepper

¼ teaspoon poultry
seasoning

2 teaspoons grated lemon
peel

6 cups *Kellogg's Corn Flakes®* Cereal

1¼ cups chicken broth

1 In 2-quart saucepan, cook sausage, onions and celery until meat is no longer pink and vegetables are crisp-tender. Drain. Add remaining ingredients, mixing only until combined. Place in 1½-quart casserole dish coated with cooking spray. Cover with lid or foil.

2 Bake at 350°F for 45 minutes or until thoroughly heated. Remove lid or foil the last 15 minutes to brown surface. Serve hot.

CHEESE STICKS

MAKES 6 SERVINGS (2 STICKS EACH)
PREP TIME: 15 MINUTES **TOTAL TIME:** 23 MINUTES

4 cups *Kellogg's® Rice Krispies®* Cereal, crushed to 1 cup

½ teaspoon garlic salt

½ teaspoon oregano

¼ cup all-purpose flour

2 egg whites

2 tablespoons water

1 (8-ounce) package mozzarella cheese

1 Combine KELLOGG'S RICE KRISPIES cereal, garlic salt and oregano in pie plate or shallow bowl. Place flour in second pie plate or bowl. In third shallow container, beat egg whites and water with fork until thoroughly combined.

2 Cut cheese into 12 sticks approximately 2¾ inches long. Dip one stick cheese in flour, then in egg mixture, then cereal mixture. Carefully repeat dipping in egg mixture and cereal mixture to double coat completely. Place on foil-lined shallow baking pan coated with cooking spray. Coat remaining cheese using same method.

3 Bake at 400°F about 8 minutes or until cheese is soft and sticks are lightly browned. Serve hot with pizza sauce or salsa, if desired.

BRAN-TOPPED CAULIFLOWER ESCALLOP

MAKES 8 SERVINGS | PREP TIME: 30 MINUTES **TOTAL TIME:** 50 MINUTES

2 tablespoons margarine or butter, melted

¼ teaspoon garlic salt

1½ cups *Kellogg's® All-Bran® Original* or ½ cup *Kellogg's® All-Bran® Bran Buds®* Cereal

4 cups sliced cauliflower (1 medium head)

1 cube chicken bouillon

¾ cup hot water

¼ cup margarine or butter

¼ cup all-purpose flour

½ teaspoon salt

⅛ teaspoon white pepper

1 cup half-and-half

2 tablespoons chopped pimientos

1 cup sliced green onions

1 Combine the 2 tablespoons melted margarine, garlic salt and KELLOGG'S ALL-BRAN cereal. Set aside for topping.

2 Cook cauliflower in small amount of water about 10 minutes or until almost tender. Drain well. Set aside.

3 Dissolve bouillon cube in ¾ cup hot water. Set aside.

4 In 3-quart saucepan, melt the ¼ cup margarine over low heat. Stir in flour, salt and pepper. Add bouillon and half-and-half, stirring until smooth. Increase heat to medium and cook until mixture boils, stirring constantly. Remove from heat. Stir in pimientos, green onions and cauliflower. Spoon mixture into 10×6×2-inch (1½-quart) glass baking dish. Sprinkle cereal mixture evenly over top.

5 Bake at 350°F about 20 minutes or until thoroughly heated and bubbly. Serve hot.

ON THE SIDE

FINISHING TOUCHES

BANANA CARAMEL SPICE PIE

MAKES 8 SERVINGS | PREP TIME: 10 MINUTES **CHILL TIME:** 4 HOURS

1 large ripe banana, sliced

1 *Keebler® Ready Crust®* Shortbread Pie Crust

2 cups cold milk

2 (3½-ounce) packages white chocolate or vanilla flavor instant pudding & pie filling (4-serving size)

½ teaspoon cinnamon

1 (8-ounce) container non-dairy whipped topping, thawed

Caramel ice cream topping

1 Place banana slices on KEEBLER READY CRUST pie crust. In large bowl, beat milk, pudding mix and cinnamon with wire whisk for 1 minute.

2 Whisk in whipped topping. Spread over banana slices.

3 Refrigerate at least 4 hours or until set. Serve drizzled with caramel topping. Store in refrigerator.

GRASSHOPPER COOKIE PIE

MAKES 8 SERVINGS | PREP TIME: 15 MINUTES **CHILL TIME:** 3 HOURS

1 (8-ounce) package cream cheese, softened*

⅓ cup sugar

3 drops green food coloring (optional)

1 (8-ounce) tub frozen non-dairy whipped topping, thawed

1 cup *Keebler® Fudge Shoppe®* Grasshopper Fudge Mint Cookies, chopped

1 *Keebler® Ready Crust®* Chocolate Pie Crust

Soften cream cheese in microwave at HIGH for 15 to 20 seconds.

1 In large mixing bowl, beat cream cheese on medium speed of electric mixer until fluffy. Add sugar and food coloring, if desired. Beat until combined.

2 Fold in whipped topping and KEEBLER FUDGE SHOPPE cookies. Spread in KEEBLER READY CRUST pie crust.

3 Refrigerate at least 3 hours or until set. Garnish as desired. Store in refrigerator.

RED, WHITE & BLUEBERRY CREAM PIE

MAKES 8 SERVINGS | **PREP TIME:** 10 MINUTES **CHILL TIME:** 3 HOURS

1¼ cups fresh blueberries, divided

1 *Keebler® Ready Crust®* Graham Pie Crust

1 (8-ounce) package cream cheese, softened*

1 (14-ounce) can sweetened condensed milk

⅓ cup lemon juice

1 teaspoon vanilla

Sliced fresh strawberries

Soften cream cheese in microwave at high for 15 to 20 seconds.

1 Place 1 cup blueberries in KEEBLER READY CRUST pie crust.

2 In large mixing bowl, beat cream cheese on medium speed of electric mixer until fluffy. Gradually beat in sweetened condensed milk. Add lemon juice and vanilla. Beat until combined. Pour over blueberries in crust.

3 Refrigerate at least 3 hours or until set. Arrange remaining blueberries and strawberries on top. Garnish as desired. Store in refrigerator.

PEANUT BUTTER CUP COOKIE ICE CREAM PIE

MAKES 8 SERVINGS | PREP TIME: 15 MINUTES **FREEZE TIME:** 3 HOURS

½ cup creamy peanut butter

¼ cup honey

1 cup *Keebler® Chips Deluxe™* Peanut Butter Cups Cookies (about 8 cookies)

1 quart vanilla ice cream, softened

1 *Keebler® Ready Crust®* Chocolate Pie Crust

½ cup chocolate ice cream topping

1 Place large bowl in freezer.

2 In small bowl, stir together peanut butter and honey. Set aside. Coarsely chop cookies.

3 In chilled bowl, combine ice cream, peanut butter mixture and cookies. Beat on low speed of electric mixer until combined. Spread half of ice cream mixture in KEEBLER READY CRUST pie crust.

4 Drizzle with ice cream topping. Carefully spread remaining ice cream mixture on top. Freeze at least 3 hours or until firm.

5 Let stand at room temperature for 15 minutes before cutting. Garnish as desired. Store in freezer.

CHOCOLATE RASPBERRY CHEESECAKE

MAKES 8 SERVINGS

PREP TIME: 10 MINUTES **BAKE TIME:** 30 TO 35 MINUTES **CHILL TIME:** 3½ HOURS

1 (8-ounce) package cream cheese, softened*

1 (14-ounce) can sweetened condensed milk

1 egg

3 tablespoons lemon juice

½ teaspoon vanilla

1 cup fresh or frozen raspberries

1 *Keebler® Ready Crust®* Chocolate Pie Crust

CHOCOLATE GLAZE

¼ cup whipping cream

2 (1-ounce) squares semi-sweet chocolate, chopped

*Soften cream cheese in microwave at HIGH for 15 to 20 seconds.

1 In large mixing bowl, beat cream cheese on medium speed of electric mixer until fluffy. Gradually beat in sweetened condensed milk.

2 Add egg, lemon juice and vanilla, mixing until just combined.

3 Arrange raspberries in KEEBLER READY CRUST pie crust. Slowly pour cheese mixture over berries. Bake at 350°F about 30 minutes or until center is almost set. Cool for 1 hour.

4 In small saucepan, combine cream and chocolate. Cook over low heat, stirring constantly, until chocolate melts and mixture thickens slightly. Remove from heat. Pour over cheesecake. Cool for 30 minutes. Refrigerate at least 2 hours.

5 Garnish as desired. Store in refrigerator.

FROSTED LEMON BARS

MAKES 36 BARS | PREP TIME: 30 MINUTES **TOTAL TIME:** 50 MINUTES

2 cups *Kellogg's Corn Flakes®* Cereal, crushed to ½ cup, or ½ cup *Kellogg's®* Corn Flake Crumbs

1 cup all-purpose flour

⅓ cup firmly packed brown sugar

⅓ cup margarine or butter, softened

2 tablespoons all-purpose flour

¼ teaspoon salt

2 eggs, slightly beaten

1 cup firmly packed brown sugar

1½ cups flaked coconut

½ teaspoon vanilla

1 cup chopped nuts

LEMON ICING

1 cup powdered sugar

1 tablespoon margarine, melted

1 tablespoon lemon juice

1 In large mixing bowl, combine KELLOGG'S CORN FLAKES cereal, 1 cup flour, ⅓ cup brown sugar and margarine. Mix well. Press evenly in bottom of 13×9×2-inch baking pan.

2 Bake at 275°F for 10 minutes. Remove baked crust from oven. Set aside. Increase oven temperature to 350°F.

3 Mix together 2 tablespoons flour and salt. Set aside.

4 In medium mixing bowl, combine eggs, 1 cup brown sugar, coconut and vanilla. Add flour mixture and nuts. Mix well. Spread over baked crust.

5 Return to oven and bake 20 minutes or until bars are lightly browned.

6 While bars are baking, prepare Lemon Icing. Combine powdered sugar, 1 tablespoon margarine and lemon juice. Beat until smooth. After bars are baked and still warm, frost with Lemon Icing. Cool and cut into bars.

FINISHING TOUCHES

BERRY PATCH TEA CAKE

MAKES 8 SERVINGS | **PREP TIME:** 15 MINUTES **TOTAL TIME:** 50 MINUTES

2 cups *Kellogg's® All-Bran® Complete®* Wheat Flakes Cereal, crushed to coarse crumbs

½ teaspoon cinnamon

2 tablespoons margarine or butter, melted

1½ cups packaged biscuit mix

½ cup sugar

3 tablespoons shortening, softened

1 egg

¾ cup milk

1 teaspoon vanilla

½ cup all fruit jam or preserves

1 Place KELLOGG'S ALL-BRAN COMPLETE cereal in small bowl. Toss lightly with cinnamon and margarine. Set aside.

2 Measure biscuit mix, sugar, shortening, egg, milk and vanilla into large mixing bowl; beat about 1 minute or until well mixed. Pour into greased 9-inch round baking pan. Dot preserves over batter. Sprinkle cereal mixture over preserves. Cut through topping into batter at regular intervals to give a marbleized appearance.

3 Bake at 350°F about 35 minutes or until wooden pick inserted near center comes out clean. Cut into wedges to serve.

APPLE CRANBERRY PIE

MAKES 8 SERVINGS | PREP TIME: 10 MINUTES **TOTAL TIME:** 55 MINUTES

1 refrigerated rolled pie pastry

2 (21-ounce) cans apple pie filling, peach pie filling or a combination

½ cup dried cranberries

½ teaspoon almond extract or vanilla

4 *Kellogg's® Pop-Tarts®* Frosted Brown Sugar Cinnamon Toaster Pastries

¼ cup finely chopped walnuts

1 Fit pastry into 9-inch pie plate according to package directions. Crimp edges.

2 In medium bowl, stir together pie filling, cranberries and almond extract. Spoon into pastry.

3 Crumble KELLOGG'S POP-TARTS toaster pastries over top of pie. Sprinkle with nuts.

4 Bake at 375°F, loosely covered with foil, for 30 minutes. Remove foil. Bake about 15 minutes more or until golden brown. Serve warm or at room temperature.

CARAMEL APPLE PIE

MAKES 8 SERVINGS | PREP TIME: 20 MINUTES **TOTAL TIME:** 4 HOURS 20 MINUTES

⅓ cup caramel ice cream topping

1 *Keebler® Ready Crust®* Graham Cracker Pie Crust

⅓ cup chopped walnuts or pecans

1 (8-ounce) package cream cheese, softened*

½ cup sour cream

2 tablespoons sugar

2 teaspoons vanilla

½ teaspoon cinnamon

½ cup chunky applesauce

1½ cups non-dairy frozen whipped topping, thawed

Cinnamon

Soften cream cheese in microwave at HIGH for 15 to 20 seconds.

1 Spread ice cream topping in KEEBLER READY CRUST pie crust. Sprinkle with nuts.

2 In small mixing bowl, beat cream cheese on medium speed of electric mixer until fluffy. Add sour cream, sugar, vanilla and ½ teaspoon cinnamon. Beat until just combined. Stir in applesauce.

3 Fold whipped topping into cream cheese mixture. Spread over nut layer in crust. Refrigerate at least 4 hours.

4 Sprinkle with cinnamon. Store in refrigerator.

GRILLED MAPLE BANANAS FOSTER

MAKES 4 SERVINGS | PREP TIME: 10 MINUTES **TOTAL TIME:** 15 MINUTES

3 small ripe bananas

2 tablespoons brown sugar

2 tablespoons butter or margarine, melted

1 teaspoon vanilla

½ teaspoon apple pie spice or pumpkin pie spice

1⅓ cups light vanilla ice cream or frozen vanilla yogurt

1½ cups *Kellogg's® Mini-Wheats®* Frosted Maple & Brown Sugar Cereal, slightly crushed to 1¼ cups

1 Peel bananas. Cut bananas into ½-inch-thick slices. Tear off one 36×12-inch piece of heavy foil. Fold in half, making 18×12-inch rectangle of double-thick foil. Place banana in center of foil.

2 In small bowl, stir together brown sugar, butter, vanilla and spice. Spoon over bananas. Bring up sides of foil and seal on top with double fold. Seal ends with double folds.

3 Grill directly over medium heat for 5 minutes*.

4 Carefully unfold foil packet. Spoon into 4 dessert dishes. Top each with scoop of ice cream. Sprinkle with KELLOGG'S MINI-WHEATS cereal. Serve immediately.

If desired, omit grilling and bake foil packet of bananas at 375°F about 10 minutes.

GINGERED PEAR CRANBERRY CRISP

MAKES 9 SERVINGS | PREP TIME: 20 MINUTES **TOTAL TIME:** 45 MINUTES

4 medium pears, cored and thinly sliced (about 9 cups)

½ cup dried cranberries

½ cup firmly packed brown sugar, divided

⅓ cup whole wheat flour, divided

3 tablespoons finely chopped crystallized ginger

½ teaspoon cinnamon

½ teaspoon vanilla

1 cup *Kellogg's® Special K®* Vanilla Almond Cereal

2 tablespoons butter or margarine, melted

3 cups low-fat vanilla frozen yogurt (optional)

1 In 8×8×2-inch baking dish, toss together pears, cranberries, 2 tablespoons brown sugar, 2 tablespoons flour, ginger, cinnamon and vanilla.

2 In small bowl, combine remaining brown sugar, remaining flour and KELLOGG'S SPECIAL K cereal. Drizzle with butter. Mix until combined. Sprinkle over fruit mixture. Bake at 375°F for 25 minutes or until fruit is tender.

3 Serve warm with scoops of frozen yogurt, if desired.

SUGAR HONEY BAKED APPLES

MAKES 8 SERVINGS | PREP TIME: 15 MINUTES **TOTAL TIME:** 1 HOUR 5 MINUTES

8 large baking apples

1 cup *Keebler®* Honey Graham Crackers, finely crushed

¾ cup sugar

⅓ cup chopped pecans or walnuts

⅓ cup margarine or butter, melted

1 tablespoon lemon juice

1 (12-ounce) can ginger ale

1 Partially core apples, leaving bottoms intact to hold stuffing. Peel strip from top of each apple.

2 In small bowl, toss together KEEBLER cracker crumbs, sugar, nuts, margarine and lemon juice. Spoon into centers of apples. In shallow baking dish, arrange apples, cut sides up.

3 Pour ginger ale around apples. Bake at 350°F for 50 to 65 minutes or until apples are tender, spooning liquid over apples occasionally. Serve warm or chilled.

FUN FOR KIDS

CHOCOLATE SCOTCHEROOS

MAKES 24 SERVINGS | **PREP TIME:** 20 MINUTES **TOTAL TIME:** 1 HOUR 20 MINUTES

1 cup light corn syrup

1 cup sugar

1 cup creamy peanut butter

6 cups *Kellogg's® Rice Krispies® or Kellogg's® Cocoa Krispies®* Cereal

1 cup semi-sweet chocolate chips (6 ounces)

1 cup butterscotch chips

1 Place corn syrup and sugar into 3-quart saucepan. Cook over medium heat, stirring frequently, until sugar dissolves and mixture begins to boil. Remove from heat. Stir in peanut butter. Mix well. Add KELLOGG'S RICE KRISPIES cereal. Stir until well coated. Evenly press mixture into 13×9×2-inch pan coated with cooking spray. Set aside.

2 Melt chocolate and butterscotch chips together in 1-quart saucepan over low heat, stirring constantly. Spread evenly over cereal mixture. Let stand until firm. Cut into 2×1-inch bars when cool.

RICE KRISPIES® BROWNIES

MAKES 24 SERVINGS | **PREP TIME:** 15 MINUTES **TOTAL TIME:** 1 HOUR 30 MINUTES

3 cups *Kellogg's® Rice Krispies®* Cereal, crushed to ¾ cup

2 cups sugar

½ cup all-purpose flour

½ cup unsweetened cocoa powder

¼ teaspoon salt

½ cup chopped pecans

½ cup vegetable oil

3 eggs, slightly beaten

¼ cup non-fat milk

1 teaspoon vanilla

1 In large mixing bowl, combine KELLOGG'S RICE KRISPIES cereal, sugar, flour, cocoa powder, salt and pecans. Add remaining ingredients; mix only until combined. Evenly spread in 13×9×2-inch baking pan coated with cooking spray.

2 Bake at 350°F about 30 minutes or until wooden pick inserted at center comes out clean. Cool completely on wire rack before cutting into 2-inch squares. Store tightly covered at room temperature.

CUP TREATS

MAKES 12 SERVINGS | PREP TIME: 40 MINUTES **TOTAL TIME:** 40 MINUTES

3 tablespoons margarine or butter

4 cups miniature marshmallows or 1 package (10 ounces, about 40) regular marshmallows

6 cups *Kellogg's® Rice Krispies® or Kellogg's® Cocoa Krispies®* Cereal

Pudding, ice cream or frozen yogurt

1 In large saucepan, melt margarine over low heat. Add marshmallows and stir until completely melted. Remove from heat.

2 Add KELLOGG'S RICE KRISPIES cereal. Stir until well coated.

3 Divide warm mixture into 2½-inch muffin-pan cups coated with cooking spray. Shape mixture into individual cups. Cool. Remove from pans. Just before serving, fill with pudding, ice cream or frozen yogurt. Serve immediately. Store no more than 2 days at room temperature in airtight container.

MICROWAVE DIRECTIONS

In microwave-safe bowl, heat margarine and marshmallows on HIGH for 3 minutes, stirring after 2 minutes. Stir until smooth. Follow steps 2 and 3 above. Microwave cooking times may vary.

NOTES

For best results, use fresh marshmallows.
1 jar (7 ounces) marshmallow crème can be substituted for marshmallows.
Diet, reduced calorie or tub margarine is not recommended.

THE ORIGINAL
RICE KRISPIES® TREATS

MAKES 12 SERVINGS | PREP TIME: 10 MINUTES **TOTAL TIME:** 30 MINUTES

3 tablespoons margarine or butter

1 package (10 ounces, about 40) regular marshmallows or 4 cups miniature marshmallows

6 cups *Kellogg's® Rice Krispies®* Cereal

1 In large saucepan, melt margarine over low heat. Add marshmallows and stir until completely melted. Remove from heat.

2 Add KELLOGG'S RICE KRISPIES cereal. Stir until well coated.

3 Using buttered spatula or wax paper, evenly press mixture into 13×9×2-inch pan coated with cooking spray. Cut into 2-inch squares when cool. Best if served the same day. Store no more than 2 days in airtight container.

MICROWAVE DIRECTIONS

In microwave-safe bowl, heat margarine and marshmallows on HIGH for 3 minutes, stirring after 2 minutes. Stir until smooth. Follow steps 2 and 3 above. Microwave cooking times may vary.

NOTES

For best results, use fresh marshmallows.

1 jar (7 ounce) marshmallow crème can be substituted for marshmallows.

Diet, reduced calorie or tub margarine is not recommended. Store no more than 2 days at room temperature in airtight container.

To freeze, place in layers separated by wax paper in airtight container. Freeze for up to 6 weeks. Let stand at room temperature for 15 minutes before serving.

FUN FOR KIDS

CHOCOLATE YUMMIES

MAKES 36 SERVINGS | **PREP TIME:** 20 MINUTES **TOTAL TIME:** 1 HOUR 20 MINUTES

7 sheets *Keebler®* Original Graham Crackers*

2½ cups miniature marshmallows

2 cups semi-sweet chocolate chips

⅔ cup light corn syrup

3 tablespoons butter or margarine

½ cup chunky peanut butter

3 cups *Kellogg's® Rice Krispies®* Cereal

*Each cracker sheet measures about 5×2 inches and is scored into 4 pieces.

1 Coat 13×9×2-inch microwave-safe dish with cooking spray. Arrange KEEBLER graham crackers in a single layer over bottom of dish, breaking crackers as needed to fit. Sprinkle marshmallows evenly over crackers.

2 Microwave on HIGH 1 minute or until marshmallows are puffy. Remove from microwave. Cool completely.

3 In 2-quart microwave-safe mixing bowl, combine chocolate chips, corn syrup and butter. Microwave on HIGH about 1½ minutes or until chocolate is melted, stirring every 30 seconds. Stir in peanut butter. Add KELLOGG'S RICE KRISPIES cereal, mixing until combined.

4 Evenly spread mixture over marshmallows. Cover and refrigerate about 1 hour or until firm. Cut and store in airtight container in refrigerator.

CONVENTIONAL DIRECTIONS

Follow step 1 above using 13×9×2-inch baking dish coated with cooking spray. Bake at 375°F about 7 minutes or until marshmallows are puffy. Cool completely. In medium saucepan, combine chocolate chips, corn syrup and butter. Cook stirring constantly, over medium-low heat until melted. Remove from heat. Stir in peanut butter. Add cereal, mixing until combined. Complete as in step 4 above.

FUN FOR KIDS

UPSIDE-DOWN CONFETTI TREATS

MAKES 12 SERVINGS | **PREP TIME:** 10 MINUTES **TOTAL TIME:** 30 MINUTES

½ cup miniature candy-coated semi-sweet chocolate pieces

3 tablespoons butter or margarine

1 package (10 ounces, about 40) regular marshmallows or 4 cups miniature marshmallows

6 cups *Kellogg's® Rice Krispies®* Cereal

1 Coat 13×9×2-inch pan with cooking spray. Evenly sprinkle candy on bottom of pan. Set aside.

2 In large saucepan, melt butter over low heat. Add marshmallows and stir until completely melted. Remove from heat.

3 Add KELLOGG'S RICE KRISPIES cereal. Stir until well coated.

4 Using buttered spatula or wax paper, evenly press mixture over candy in pan. Cool. Cut into 2-inch squares. Serve candy-side up. Best if served the same day.

FROSTED CHEWS

MAKES 24 SERVINGS | PREP TIME: 20 MINUTES **TOTAL TIME:** 50 MINUTES

1 cup corn syrup

1 cup sugar

1 cup creamy peanut butter

8 cups *Kellogg's® Special K®* Crispy Rice Cereal

1 cup semi-sweet chocolate chips (6-ounce package)

1 cup butterscotch chips (6-ounce package)

1 Combine corn syrup and sugar in medium-size saucepan. Stir to combine. Cook over medium heat, stirring frequently, until mixture begins to bubble. Remove from heat. Stir in peanut butter.

2 Add KELLOGG'S SPECIAL K cereal. Stir until evenly coated. With back of tablespoon, press mixture evenly and firmly in bottom of buttered 13×9×2-inch pan. Cool.

3 Melt chocolate and butterscotch chips together in small saucepan over very low heat, stirring constantly. Spread evenly over cereal mixture. Cut bars when cool.

FUN FOR KIDS

PIZZA TREATS

MAKES 12 SERVINGS | PREP TIME: 15 MINUTES **TOTAL TIME:** 35 MINUTES

3 tablespoons butter or margarine

1 package (10 ounces, about 40) regular marshmallows or 4 cups miniature marshmallows

6 cups *Kellogg's® Rice Krispies®* or *Kellogg's® Cocoa Krispies®* Cereal

Strawberry jam

Canned frosting

Fruit roll-ups, cut into 1¼-inch circles

Multi-colored sprinkles

1 In large saucepan, melt butter over low heat. Add marshmallows and stir until completely melted. Remove from heat.

2 Add KELLOGG'S RICE KRISPIES cereal. Stir until well coated.

3 Using buttered spatula or wax paper, evenly press mixture into 12-inch pizza pan coated with cooking spray. Cool.

4 Spread strawberry jam on top for "tomato sauce." Carefully spread frosting over jam for "cheese." Add fruit roll-up circles for "pepperoni." Top with sprinkles. Cut into slices to serve. Best if served the same day.

MICROWAVE DIRECTIONS

In microwave-safe bowl, heat butter and marshmallows on HIGH for 3 minutes, stirring after 2 minutes. Stir until smooth. Follow steps 2 through 4 above. Microwave cooking times may vary.

NOTES

For best results, use fresh marshmallows.
1 jar (7 ounces) marshmallow crème can be substituted for marshmallows.
Diet, reduced calorie or tub margarine is not recommended.
Store no more than 2 days at room temperature in airtight container.
To freeze, place in layers separated by wax paper in airtight container. Freeze for up to 6 weeks. Let stand at room temperature for 15 minutes before serving.

GIANT REMOTE CONTROL

MAKES 6 SERVINGS | **PREP TIME:** 20 MINUTES **TOTAL TIME:** 40 MINUTES

3 tablespoons butter or margarine

1 package (10 ounces, about 40) regular marshmallows or 4 cups miniature marshmallows

6 cups *Kellogg's® Rice Krispies®* or *Kellogg's® Cocoa Krispies®* Cereal

Canned frosting or decorating gel

Assorted candies

1 In large saucepan, melt butter over low heat. Add marshmallows and stir until completely melted. Remove from heat.

2 Add KELLOGG'S RICE KRISPIES cereal. Stir until well coated.

3 Using buttered spatula or wax paper, evenly press mixture into 13×9×2-inch pan coated with cooking spray. Cool. Decorate with frosting and/or candies for control buttons. To serve, cut into 2-inch squares. Best if served the same day.

MICROWAVE DIRECTIONS

In microwave-safe bowl, heat butter and marshmallows on HIGH for 3 minutes, stirring after 2 minutes. Stir until smooth. Follow steps 2 and 3 above. Microwave cooking times may vary.

NOTES

For best results, use fresh marshmallows.

1 jar (7 ounces) marshmallow crème can be substituted for marshmallows.

Diet, reduced calorie or tub margarine is not recommended.

Store no more than 2 days at room temperature in airtight container.

To freeze, place in layers separated by wax paper in airtight container. Freeze for up to 6 weeks. Let stand at room temperature for 15 minutes before serving.

MOTHER'S DAY MUG

MAKES 4 SERVINGS | PREP TIME: 20 MINUTES **TOTAL TIME:** 40 MINUTES

3 tablespoons butter or margarine

1 package (10 ounces, about 40) regular marshmallows or 4 cups miniature marshmallows

6 cups *Kellogg's® Rice Krispies®* Cereal

Canned frosting or decorating gel

1 In large saucepan, melt butter over low heat. Add marshmallows and stir until completely melted. Remove from heat.

2 Add KELLOGG'S RICE KRISPIES cereal. Stir until well coated.

3 Cool slightly. Using buttered hands, shape cereal mixture into mug shapes, reserving small portions of cereal mixture for handles. Attach one handle to each mug, securing with frosting. Decorate with additional frosting. Best if served the same day.

MICROWAVE DIRECTIONS

In microwave-safe bowl heat butter and marshmallows on HIGH for 3 minutes, stirring after 2 minutes. Stir until smooth. Follow steps 2 and 3 above. Microwave cooking times may vary.

NOTES

For best results, use fresh marshmallows.

1 jar (7 ounces) marshmallow crème can be substituted for marshmallows.

Diet, reduced calorie or tub margarine is not recommended.

Store no more than 2 days at room temperature in airtight container.

To freeze, place in single layer on wax paper in airtight container. Freeze for up to 6 weeks. Let stand at room temperature for 15 minutes before serving.

FUN FOR KIDS

SUMMER BALLOON TREATS

MAKES 15 SERVINGS | **PREP TIME:** 20 MINUTES **TOTAL TIME:** 40 MINUTES

3 tablespoons butter or margarine

1 package (10 ounces, about 40) regular marshmallows or 4 cups miniature marshmallows

6 cups *Kellogg's® Rice Krispies® or Kellogg's® Cocoa Krispies®* Cereal

Canned frosting or decorating gel

Food coloring

Assorted candies

Licorice strings

1 In large saucepan, melt butter over low heat. Add marshmallows and stir until completely melted. Remove from heat.

2 Add KELLOGG'S RICE KRISPIES cereal. Stir until well coated.

3 Using buttered spatula or wax paper, evenly press mixture into 15×10×1-inch pan coated with cooking spray. Cool slightly. Using cookie cutters coated with cooking spray, cut into balloon shapes. Decorate with frosting and/or candies. Add licorice strings for balloon strings. Best if served the same day.

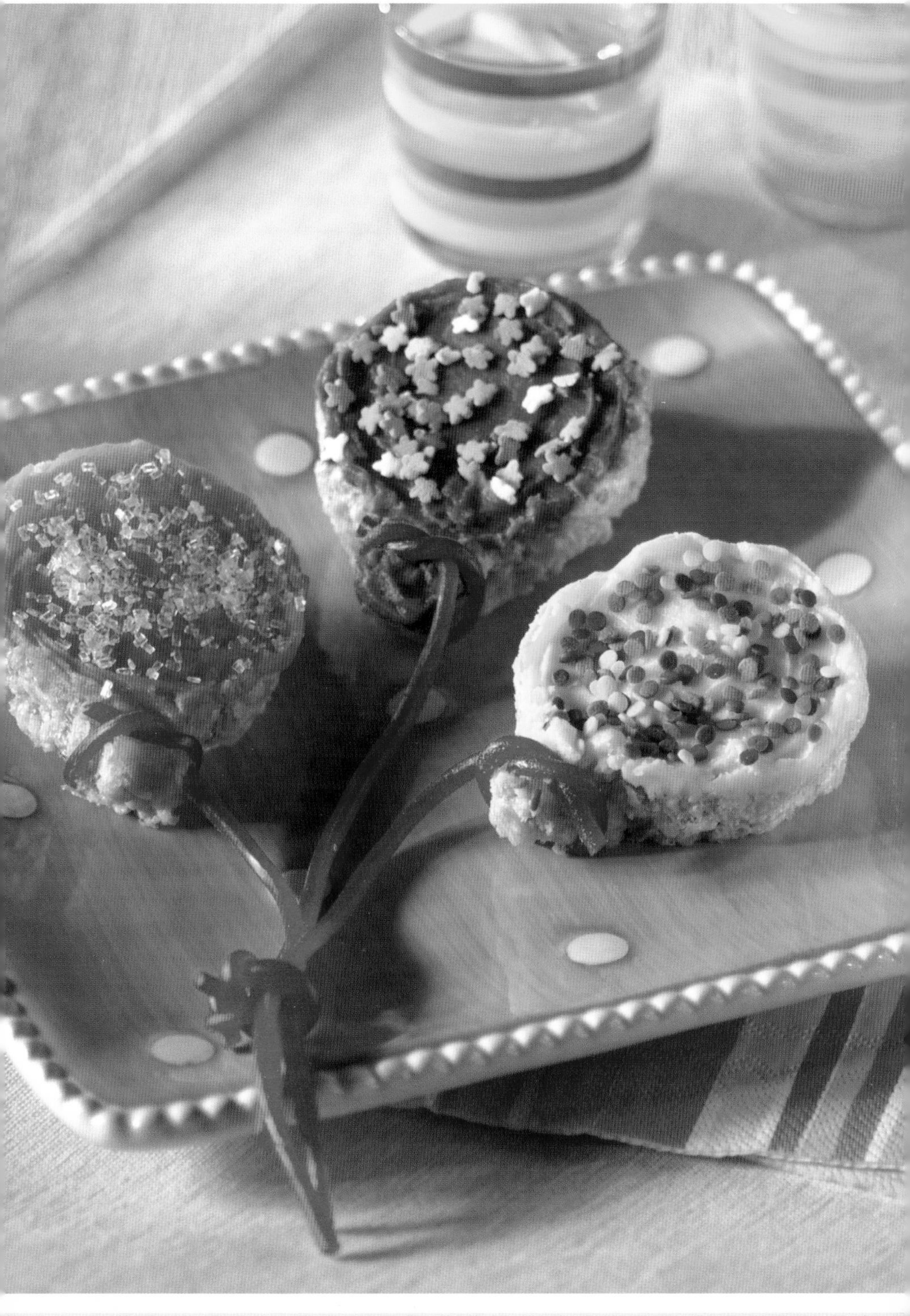

TO CLOSE
INSERT TAB HERE

X'S AND O'S TREATS

MAKES 18 SERVINGS | PREP TIME: 20 MINUTES **TOTAL TIME:** 40 MINUTES

3 tablespoons butter or margarine

1 package (10 ounces, about 40) regular marshmallows or 4 cups miniature marshmallows

6 cups *Kellogg's® Rice Krispies®* or *Kellogg's® Cocoa Krispies®* Cereal

Canned frosting or decorating gel

Food coloring

Assorted candies

1 In large saucepan, melt butter over low heat. Add marshmallows and stir until completely melted. Remove from heat.

2 Add KELLOGG'S RICE KRISPIES cereal. Stir until well coated.

3 Using buttered spatula or wax paper, evenly press mixture into 15×10×1-inch pan coated with cooking spray. Cool slightly. Using cookie cutters coated with cooking spray, cut into "X" and "O" shapes. Decorate with frosting and/or candies. Best if served the same day.

MICROWAVE DIRECTIONS

In microwave-safe bowl, heat butter and marshmallows on HIGH for 3 minutes, stirring after 2 minutes. Stir until smooth. Follow steps 2 and 3 above. Microwave cooking times may vary.

NOTES

For best results, use fresh marshmallows.
1 jar (7 ounces) marshmallow crème can be substituted for marshmallows.
Diet, reduced calorie or tub margarine is not recommended.
Store no more than 2 days at room temperature in airtight container.
To freeze, place in single layer on wax paper in airtight container. Freeze for up to 6 weeks. Let stand at room temperature for 15 minutes before serving.

E

Entrées

F

G

H

K

INDEX

METRIC CONVERSION CHART

VOLUME MEASUREMENTS (dry)

1/8 teaspoon = 0.5 mL
1/4 teaspoon = 1 mL
1/2 teaspoon = 2 mL
3/4 teaspoon = 4 mL
1 teaspoon = 5 mL
1 tablespoon = 15 mL
2 tablespoons = 30 mL
1/4 cup = 60 mL
1/3 cup = 75 mL
1/2 cup = 125 mL
2/3 cup = 150 mL
3/4 cup = 175 mL
1 cup = 250 mL
2 cups = 1 pint = 500 mL
3 cups = 750 mL
4 cups = 1 quart = 1 L

VOLUME MEASUREMENTS (fluid)

1 fluid ounce (2 tablespoons) = 30 mL
4 fluid ounces (1/2 cup) = 125 mL
8 fluid ounces (1 cup) = 250 mL
12 fluid ounces (1 1/2 cups) = 375 mL
16 fluid ounces (2 cups) = 500 mL

WEIGHTS (mass)

1/2 ounce = 15 g
1 ounce = 30 g
3 ounces = 90 g
4 ounces = 120 g
8 ounces = 225 g
10 ounces = 285 g
12 ounces = 360 g
16 ounces = 1 pound = 450 g

DIMENSIONS

1/16 inch = 2 mm
1/8 inch = 3 mm
1/4 inch = 6 mm
1/2 inch = 1.5 cm
3/4 inch = 2 cm
1 inch = 2.5 cm

OVEN TEMPERATURES

250°F = 120°C
275°F = 140°C
300°F = 150°C
325°F = 160°C
350°F = 180°C
375°F = 190°C
400°F = 200°C
425°F = 220°C
450°F = 230°C

BAKING PAN SIZES

Utensil	Size in Inches/Quarts	Metric Volume	Size in Centimeters
Baking or Cake Pan (square or rectangular)	8×8×2	2 L	20×20×5
	9×9×2	2.5 L	23×23×5
	12×8×2	3 L	30×20×5
	13×9×2	3.5 L	33×23×5
Loaf Pan	8×4×3	1.5 L	20×10×7
	9×5×3	2 L	23×13×7
Round Layer Cake Pan	8×1½	1.2 L	20×4
	9×1½	1.5 L	23×4
Pie Plate	8×1¼	750 mL	20×3
	9×1¼	1 L	23×3
Baking Dish or Casserole	1 quart	1 L	—
	1½ quart	1.5 L	—
	2 quart	2 L	—